BIRDS OF THE WORLD
BIRDS OF PREY

BIRDS OF THE WORLD
BIRDS OF PREY

JOHN P.S. MACKENZIE

KEY PORTER BOOKS

Cataloguing in Publication Data

Mackenzie, John P.S.
        Birds of prey

(Birds of the world)
Includes index.
ISBN 1-55013-010-2 (bound)
ISBN 1-55013-803-0 (pbk.)

1. Birds of prey. – Pictorial works I. Title. II. Series:
Mackenzie, John P.S. Birds of the World.

QL696.F3M24   1986   598'.91'0222   C86-094246-5

Key Porter Books Limited
70 The Esplanade
Toronto, Ontario
Canada M5E 1R2

Typesetting: Computer Composition of Canada, Inc.

Distributed in the United States by Firefly Books

Printed and bound in Hong Kong

97 98 99 00 6 5 4 3 2 1

Front cover: The largest of the falcons, the handsome Gyrfalcon is seldom seen south of the Arctic Circle.
Back cover: The magnificent Bald Eagle is found only in North America. Its numbers have been drastically reduced due to pesticide poisoning, but it is still seen frequently along the northern Pacific coast.
Page 2: Andean Condor (*Vultur gryphus*). This huge bird has a ten-foot wingspan and four-foot length. It searches for carrion in the mountains, often soaring great distances and storing the food in its stomach.
Pages 4-5: Gyrfalcon (*Falco rusticolus*). A Gyrfalcon nest, or eyrie, overlooking Arctic waters. Controversy exists about whether first-year or "passage" birds should be captured for export to Middle East falconers.

CONTENTS

Left. Goshawk (*Accipiter gentilis*) An extremely rare forest dweller, the Northern Goshawk is a close-to-the-ground hunter and the largest of the accipiters, a hawk grouping which also includes the Sharp-shinned and Cooper's hawks.

Auger Buzzard (*Buteo rufofuscus*) The Auger Buzzard is a mid-sized hawk living mostly in the highlands of Africa, but it can also be seen in farming areas.

American Kestrel (formerly Sparrow Hawk) (*Falco sparverius*) Kestrels are often overlooked in urban areas, but can be located by the cry, a staccato series of *kee, kee, kee*, high-pitched and shrill.

INTRODUCTION

Golden Eagle (*Aquila chrysaëtos*) Golden Eagles, which have a wingspan of over seven feet, can still be found in the more mountainous western Arctic. Their nest is usually on a cliff, made of sticks and lined with softer material. Their favorite food is ground squirrels.

"He clasps the crag with crooked hands;
Close to the sun in lonely lands,
Ring'd with the azure world he stands.
The wrinkled sea beneath him crawls;
He watches from his mountain walls
And like a thunderbolt he falls."

Alfred, Lord Tennyson, "The Eagle"

Tennyson's words present a vivid impression of the grandeur and power of the eagle and its surroundings. His description also reflects a sense of the freedom and control in the air that humans have been trying to achieve since Icarus plunged into the sea. Eagles and other birds of prey, more than any other family of birds, stir in us a sense of our inadequacy because we are unable to lift ourselves into the air by our own power and soar at will.

Tennyson not only captures the eagle's power and ability, he suggests the reason for those qualities. In falling "like a thunderbolt," the eagle's aim is to kill for its own sustenance and for that of its young – a characteristic it shares with most birds of prey. This group also includes families with widely differing habits and habitats. Some strike their living prey with deadly talons, while others, like the Bald Eagle which is revered as the symbol of the United States, live almost entirely on dead fish found along the shore. Vultures, of course, feed entirely on dead animals.

The term *birds of prey* is commonly accepted to refer to owls and the group of birds known as *falconiformes*. This group is divided into five families representing some 298 species worldwide. The families of *falconiformes* are the American vultures (seven species), the Secretary Bird (one species), hawks, which include the eagles (226 species), the Osprey (one species) and the falcons (sixty-three species). The characteristics that link this group are their almost total reliance on insects and the flesh and innards of other animals for food, their bills which hook down sharply at the tip, the fleshy cere on the top of the bill through which the nostrils open, and their powerful feet with long claws and opposable hind toes. Owls, which have all the same features except the fleshy cere but are soft feathered, were once considered part of the same order.

Birds of prey is not an entirely apt or exclusive description of the order of *falconiformes* for there are many other families, embracing thousands of species, that take all or part of their sustenance by preying on other animals, fish or insects. Indeed, they include every species that does not rely entirely on seeds, plants or fruit. Among them are the wading birds, some ducks, herons, crows, jays, shrikes, thrushes, warblers, vireos, woodpeckers, ocean birds, gulls and many others. Even seed-eaters such as the finches feed almost entirely on insects during the nesting season in order to increase the protein for their eggs and to feed their young. However, the term *birds of prey* has been ascribed only to owls and *falconiformes*.

From earliest times, birds have played an important part in mythology as omens and augurs of the proper course to take in war or civil administration, as objects of worship, as forecasters of weather and harvests and as symbols of authority. The eagle has been used symbolically more than any other bird. Doves and swans have been adopted as symbols of gentleness; the woodpecker has been associated with magic, and the pelican with piety; the eagle and other large hawks have been widely used as symbols of authority. This distinction survives in the generalized descriptions of factions favoring strength and compromise as "hawks" and "doves". The eagle has been adopted as the national symbol of such countries as Russia, Germany, Turkey, Austria and Poland as well as the United States. It came to Europe as an emblem during the Middle Ages from the Middle East where the Byzantines had depicted it with two heads, both crowned. In many countries the eagle is, or was, used ritually as the crown of the scepter and other instruments of royal authority. In Napoleonic France, the eagle was the rallying point for each regiment.

The use of birds of prey or raptors for killing other birds was practiced in China as long ago as 2000 B.C., making falconry possibly the world's most ancient sport. The sport eventually became highly structured and dominated by tradition; certain species of raptors could be used only by people of various strata of society. Eagles were reserved for emperors and Gyrfalcons for kings, while princes were limited to the Peregrine Falcon, priests to Sparrow Hawks and peasants to kestrels. The hooded, or blindfolded, raptor was generally carried on the wrist, which was protected by a heavy leather glove. The bird was restrained by jesses, or leather thongs, which its owner released when the dogs flushed the quarry. The falcon then flew above its victim and stooped, or dived, on it, striking the back with its talons. The falcon was retrieved by swinging a piece of meat on a thong and calling loudly.

Falconry has survived into our time, although it is no longer associated with rank or class. While several accipiters and buteos, such as Ferruginous, Red-tailed, Rough-legged and Broad-winged Hawks, have been trained to the lure, the large falcons provide the greatest excitement, since their speed and grace surpass those of all other hawks. In addition, owls and even birds as small as shrikes have been trained. In many countries young people start with a small falcon such as a kestrel or small accipiter and graduate to larger hawks. Competitions are arranged by falconers' clubs, somewhat similar in form to retriever trials. Many falconers practice alone simply for the pleasure of experiencing the results of long training and patience. Trained birds become very attached to their trainers; in many cases they will travel unhooded and unconstrained, simply perched on the trainer's shoulder. Since, in the absence of disease or accident, hawks are long-lived birds, the association may last for many years.

In parts of Asia, and perhaps elsewhere, falconry has a more practical purpose. There, large hawks such as the Golden Eagle have been trained to kill animals such as gazelles, foxes, goats and wolves for food and fur. One eagle is said to have taken fourteen wolves in a single day.

Most of the raptors are extremely efficient in flight, particularly the broad-winged families such as buteos and vultures, which, under reasonable thermal conditions, can maintain altitude without flapping. This ability to soar allows them to remain aloft without effort during the daylight hours while searching for food or migrating. For other *falconiformes*, such as falcons, with a lower ratio of wing size to weight, flying requires more effort. As a consequence, these families tend to hunt closer to the ground or from elevated perches.

Most birds of prey have stiff feathers, particularly the primary, or flight, feathers. A Bald Eagle taking to the air can make a lot of noise as the air rushes through its flight feathers. In a stoop, or dive, a Peregrine Falcon can be heard for some distance. Owls, on the other hand, have soft feathers and fly almost silently.

Birds of prey migrate when necessary, and only as far as necessary. Many tropical hawks tend to be sedentary while those nesting in the North move to moderate climates in winter. Unlike ducks, hawks do not maintain any formation; they just move in the same direction at the same time. But hawk migration can be spectacular. In order to soar and cover long distances without much effort, hawks follow conventional and rather narrow routes along the sides of hills and mountain ranges where thermal currents are strong. Unlike most birds, which migrate during the night, hawks fly only during the daylight hours of rising air. They avoid long passages over water and in Western Europe concentrate on the Iberian Peninsula, crossing the Mediterranean from Gibraltar to North Africa. In eastern North

America, vast numbers of hawks follow the western shore of Lake Ontario via the Niagara Escarpment. At high points there, one can see thousands of birds on a good flying day. The best-known spot on the eastern flyway is at Hawk Mountain in Pennsylvania, where many of the migrants fly below the level of the observers.

Under normal conditions, birds of prey tend to live a long time. Most reach breeding maturity slowly. The California Condor, for example, attempts its first nesting at the age of six or later. Birds of prey lay only a few eggs, seldom more than two or three in a clutch. The eggs usually require a long incubation period, and in many cases, the young need more than a year of feeding and care by the parents. The California Condor nests only on alternate years. Most hawks build large nests in trees, returning each year to the same site to add to the old nest. Bald Eagle nests may become many feet high and eventually so heavy that they topple the tree in which they are built. Falcons build their nests on ledges high up on cliffs or on the roofs of tall buildings.

From the earliest times, man has persecuted raptors – mostly because of a misunderstanding about what the birds eat. Most hawks feed on rodents, rabbits and other small animals. Others such as the Osprey and the Bald Eagle live on fish, usually coarse fish. Accipiters such as the Goshawk, Cooper's Hawk and the Sharp-shinned Hawk feed mostly on small birds, game birds and the occasional chicken. The predations of the few chicken-thieves have, however, given all hawks a bad reputation, and they have been shot and trapped indiscriminately as a result.

In North America all raptors are now protected, but it was not always so. In 1921 Dr. G. Gordon Hewitt, then Dominion entomologist and consulting zoologist for the government of Canada, published a major work on the conservation of wildlife. In discussing the Goshawk, Cooper's Hawk, the Sharp-shinned Hawk and the Great Horned Owl he said, ''Their protection cannot be urged, and they should be treated as noxious predatory animals.'' This was written before it was accepted that interference with natural predation tends quite quickly, through overpopulation and resulting undernourishment, to weaken the species being protected. In areas where wolves and coyotes are eliminated, for example, the population of White-tailed Deer quickly destroys its own habitat.

Almost everywhere in Europe full protection of raptors is provided by law, but legal protection does not necessarily prevent destruction of birds, not only birds of prey. Songbirds are netted extensively for food in Italy. In the United Kingdom, where pheasant and partridge are reared on shooting estates, keepers shoot birds of prey whenever they can.

More serious now than shooting is the effect of insecticides on raptors. Relying on the flesh of other living forms, which themselves feed largely on insecticide-treated foliage, the raptor is at the end of the food chain. Toxic substances tend to remain in the fat and bones of birds, and although they are unlikely to be destroyed directly, their reproductive capacities are undermined. Many sterile eggs are laid, and those that are fertile have thin shells which are easily broken in the nest. During the 1960s the populations of many European and American species were drastically reduced. Early in the 1970s, the use of DDT was banned in North America. The Bald Eagle, which had been listed officially as endangered, began to recover as did the Brown Pelican in Florida and California. In South America, DDT is still used extensively, and many species that nest in the North remain exposed during the winter. European countries now control the use of hydrocarbons in agriculture as do meat-exporting countries. The banning of the use of highly toxic chemicals does not take place in response to the danger to birds or even humans, but usually when the products of agriculture are so contaminated that they are not acceptable. Despite much research, little is yet known about the long-term effects of toxicity, but it is encouraging that some recovery has taken place.

Secretary Bird (*Saggittarius serpentarius*) The Secretary Bird's long soft crest feathers are particularly noticeable when blown about by the wind.

SECRETARY BIRD

Secretary Bird (*Saggittarius serpentarius*) A long-legged, long-tailed bird of the African plains, the Secretary Bird seldom flies. Instead, it walks and runs about in search of its prey.

There are several "families" of birds that are represented by only one species. Of these, two are members of the *falconiforme* order of birds: the Osprey and the Secretary Bird. The latter is singled out because it differs so greatly from all other hawks in having extraordinarily long legs and an unusually long, stiff tail, and in being able to chase its prey on foot.

The Secretary Bird gets it name from the similarity of its crest feathers to a quill pen stuck behind a clerk's ear. The bird averages about forty-five inches in length and fifty inches in height, with a wingspan of about two feet. The female is generally smaller than the male; otherwise the sexes are similar in appearance.

Although the Secretary Bird can fly strongly and is an expert at soaring – it has been seen, from aircraft, at twelve thousand feet above the ground – it usually will not take wing unless pursued. When it does fly, it makes its takeoffs and landings at a run with outstretched wings. When in flight, the bird utters a high-pitched shriek; on the ground, its voice is a low, frog-like croak.

The Secretary Bird spends most of its time striding sedately through the African grasslands in search of prey: large arthropods, for the most part, but also rodents, lizards, and the young of various creatures – including birds. The bird has a reputation as a snake-killer, but though it will take snakes when it finds them, it does not particularly seek them out.

Whatever its prey, the Secretary Bird kills with its bill or with blows of the feet, and swallows its victim whole. Its short-clawed feet, ideal for walking and for striking prey, are incapable of grasping and carrying prey.

The bird is found from the Cape of Good Hope northward throughout the savannah to the south of the Sahara, at elevations of three to six thousand feet above sea level. Its preferred range is areas of grass a foot and a half or less in height; grass more than three feet tall is avoided, as is dense brush. It is not found in true deserts, although it can live in semi-desert scrub.

The Secretary Bird can live quite well on land used for large-scale commercial farming, but cannot survive where its habitat is invaded by numerous landholders. Because such invasion is extremely widespread, the bird's numbers are decreasing throughout its range.

The nest, made of sticks, is large and flat – three to five feet across, and one foot thick, sometimes becoming wider with repeated use over a number of seasons. The bird lays one to three eggs – elongated ovals, white or blue-green in color.

The safety of the nest is less dependent upon its height above the ground than it is upon the density and thorniness of the bush or tree – usually a flat-topped acacia – in which it is built. Because the nest is vulnerable the Secretary Bird cannot breed successfully where there is a large human population.

Right. Secretary Bird (*Saggittarius serpentarius*) This bird feeds on snakes, lizards, rodents, insects, and the young of various creatures.

Secretary Bird (*Saggittarius serpentarius*) The Secretary Bird stands over four feet tall and has a wing span of about two feet.

OSPREY

Osprey (*Pandion haliaetus*) This lovely fish-eating hawk appears in small numbers in almost every part of the temperate world. Its pale head and underparts and its long wings with a backward sweep are distinctive.

The Osprey, which like the Secretary Bird is the only member of its family, is one of the most exciting of all the raptors. A large bird with a wingspan of nearly six feet, it eats only fish which it catches itself or occasionally steals from gulls or other weaker species. It fishes by rising to heights of up to a hundred feet. On sighting its prey the Osprey hovers momentarily, then plunges directly into the water feet first, usually with a great splash. It often submerges completely before it can grasp the fish in its talons. If successful, it will emerge from the water with the fish carried in line with its own body, head foremost. Ospreys are capable of rising from the water with prey as heavy as or even heavier than their own three-pound weight.

One of the Osprey's three front toes is reversible, enabling it to be used as a hind toe in securing a firm grip on the struggling fish. The prey is then taken to a favorite perch and eaten or, if the Osprey is nesting, to the nest to be fed to the young. Hunting Ospreys are often harassed by eagles, which force them to release their prey which the eagles then seize.

The underside of the Osprey is white, sometimes with bars; the upper parts are dark; the tail is barred dark and white. The wings are long and slender with a distinct backward sweep from the elbow. When the Osprey is flying about with gulls it can often be overlooked for its flight pattern and color are somewhat similar to the gulls'.

Living on fish as they do, Ospreys are often shot on rivers used for sport fishing. There is no question that they can do much damage at fish hatcheries, where they become fearless, but on most streams they feed largely on coarse fish such as chub and carp which compete for food with game fish. As a result of shooting and of long exposure to pesticide-affected fish, the numbers of Osprey have been much reduced, but in recent years some recovery has taken place in most parts of the world.

Ospreys nest either singly or in scattered groups in suitable areas, usually in trees close to the water. In southern areas mangroves are favored. They do, on occasion, nest on the ground or on manmade structures such as utility poles. Over the years the nest becomes an enormous untidy affair, consisting of sticks as large as the Osprey can carry.

Writing of his experiences in the southern United States in the mid-nineteenth century, the great artist and ornithologist John James Audubon quaintly describes the courtship of the Osprey. "As soon as the females make their appearance . . . the love-season commences, and soon after, incubation takes place. The loves of these birds are conducted in a different way from those of the other Falcons. The males are seen playing through the air amongst themselves, chasing each other in sport, or sailing by the side or after the female which they have selected, uttering cries of joy and exultation, alighting on the branches of the tree on which their last year's nest is yet seen remaining, and doubtless congratulating each other on finding their home again. Their caresses are mutual. They begin to augment their habitation, or to repair the injuries which it may have sustained during the winter, and are seen sailing together toward the shores, to collect the drifted seaweeds with which they line the nest anew." While modern observers might doubt that birds are capable of the emotions Audubon so delightfully attributes to them, his description is entirely accurate.

The Osprey is unusual in that its distribution is almost worldwide. It appears in almost every temperate area with the exception of New Zealand and the Hawaiian Islands. In Europe the Osprey has become scarce. In the United Kingdom it disappeared entirely about 1900, although one pair was seen in the early 1950s in Scotland, where Osprey had not nested for fifty years. The location of this first nest was kept a secret to protect it from egg collectors and other intruders. Since the 1950s, the number of Ospreys in Scotland has increased modestly although second-generation birds have laid infertile eggs due to insecticide poisoning.

Osprey (*Pandion haliaetus*) A female Osprey is joined at the nest by a male, which flies in with a stick to add to the growing pile.

Left. Osprey (*Pandion haliaetus*) Osprey live entirely on fish which they take by plunging into the water with half-folded wings. They grasp the living fish in their talons and carry it aloft, shaking the water from their feathers.

Osprey (*Pandion haliaetus*) The nest of the Osprey is usually built in a prominent place either overhanging or close to water. It may be a single nest or part of a loose colony spread over a wide area.

Osprey (*Pandion haliaetus*) In North America, Osprey breed from Alaska to Newfoundland, south to the Gulf Coast and Florida. They also breed in North Africa, Eurasia, the East Indies and Australia.

AMERICAN VULTURES

Left. Osprey (*Pandion haliaetus*) This huge Osprey nest has been built on top of a utility pole. To discourage this practice when it becomes a nuisance, the utility companies sometimes erect poles with a flat top nearby as a suitable alternative.

Andean Condor (*Vultur gryphus*) This enormous bird has a wingspan of some ten feet. It is now rare, the remaining birds living in the Andes of Columbia, Chile, Equador and Peru.

The seven species of American vultures represent a distinct family of the *falconiformes* order. They are only remotely related to the Old World vultures, which are, schematically, part of the family of accipiters. Unlike the Old World family, American vultures have rather weak feet and short claws unsuited for grasping and tearing flesh. Since the bill is also weak, the bird can feed only on small or rotted carcasses. I once watched Turkey Vultures working ineffectually at the carcass of a newly dead sheep. They were able to attack only the eyes. A week later they had more success.

One member of this family, the Andean Condor, is the world's largest flying bird. It has a wingspan of about twelve feet and weighs twenty to twenty-five pounds. This species is frequently shot by villagers in Peru. It is also used there in a ceremony called the *arranque del condor* in which it is suspended from a frame. Horsemen ride past, punching the bird with their fists until it is dead.

The California Condor, the largest North American bird, has a wingspan of about nine feet. It is black except for a white lining on the underside of its wings. Its numbers are now reduced to about four dozen individuals, and it is probably on the road to extinction.

While the California Condor population has probably never been large, the present remnant represents only a small fraction of what it was before California was settled by Europeans. In the nineteenth century the bird's range extended intermittently from British Columbia to Baja California. Today all remaining California Condors live in a range of horseshoe-shaped mountains north of Los Angeles extending from the coast to the western slope of the Sierra Nevadas. The continuing existence of the few remaining birds has depended on the efforts of the United States Fish and Wildlife Service, the State of California and the National Audubon Society.

Shooting reduced the number of California Condors precipitously, but the introduction of sheep and cattle into its range has aggravated its problems. Each bird must consume about two pounds of meat per day, usually eaten while fairly fresh. Dead cattle are useful for food, as are deer, elk, squirrels and antelope, and do provide food during the winter. In summer, however, livestock mortality is low, and ranchers tend to remove the carcasses of dead beasts. The problem is aggravated for breeding birds that cannot fly far from the nest in search of food during the long period of incubation and rearing of their single chick. This period is so long that California Condors nest only every second year. Unintentional interference from a sonic boom, blasting or even a truck a mile away may cause a sitting bird to leap off the nest, often destroying the egg or young.

To protect these birds, the carcasses of animals killed on roads have been placed in appropriate places. This practice has met with considerable success. Sensitive areas have been closed to vehicles and hikers, and the encroachment of cottages and oil rigs has been discouraged. Despite these efforts, the remaining population of California Condors is aging and failing to expand.

The vulture seen through most of North America is the Turkey Vulture. The Black Vulture is more widely distributed in the South and in South America. The two species can be distinguished by the lighter color and longer tail of the American Vulture. Both species are distinguishable from other soaring birds by their habit of holding their wings well above the horizontal. In the northern end of the range, they are quite rare, but in winter, especially in Florida, one can see hundreds in the air at the same time. There it is always surprising that such a large population can be sustained, although it is likely that animals killed on the roads are the principal food supply.

Vultures are noted for their keen eyesight. When one bird finds a carcass the message passes visually from one bird to another and soon they come from all directions. While it is likely that vultures spread disease, their role as scavengers tends to limit infection from corpses that would otherwise become putrid.

Turkey Vulture (*Cathartes aura*) By using thermal uplift, this vulture can soar for hours without flapping its wings. It can be recognized by its long tail and by its habit of holding its wings in a V well above the horizontal.

Turkey Vulture (*Cathartes aura*) The black face of this young Turkey Vulture
will soon turn red. Turkey Vultures never build a nest but lay their eggs in
some sheltered place, usually on the ground, but sometimes on a stump or
in a crevice. It lays two eggs.

Turkey Vulture (*Cathartes aura*) This bird is not strong enough to do its own killing. Instead, it soars in search of carrion, relying on its keen vision rather than its strength for finding its food.

Left. King Vulture (*Sarcoramphus papa*) A large creamy-colored vulture with black flight feathers, the King ranges from southern Mexico to Argentina. It flies alone or in pairs, almost always at a considerable height and apart from other vultures.

Black Vulture (*Coragyps atratus*) A short-tailed North and South American species, this vulture cannot soar as well as the Turkey Vulture. It therefore spends more time at perches waiting for its meal to be killed by other animals.

Turkey Vulture (*Cathartes aura*) The naked face of the Turkey Vulture is
typical of all vultures. With some species the whole neck is bare. This allows
the bird to remain relatively clean as it dips its head into the entrails of
carrion.

Andean Condor (*Vultur gryphus*) This great bird is now much reduced in numbers but, without persecution by man, would stand a chance of survival in remote areas of the mountains. It is, however, often shot or captured.

Turkey Vulture (*Cathartes aura*) This common vulture nests from southern Canada through all of South America. It has a long tail and bi-colored wings, dark at the front and paler in the flight feathers.

Right. California Condor (*Gymnogyps californianus*) The California Condor, the largest of North American birds, is on the verge of extinction, with fewer than ten birds remaining in the wild. Since captive birds have never bred, the chance of recovery is remote.

FALCONS

Left. Andean Condor (*Vultur gryphus*) This glossy black bird is distinguished by the white ruff at the base of its bald head and neck.

Gyrfalcon (*Falco rusticolus*) This large powerful falcon lives in the northern tundra around the world, and occasionally wanders south in winter to the United Kingdom, the Baltic and the northern United States. It feeds almost entirely on seabirds.

Falcons have a unique place among the raptors, indeed among all birds. They carry an aura of mystery and remoteness for, with the exception of the American Kestrel, they are seldom seen in settled areas of North America. But it is their speed that captures the imagination and invokes wonder. To see a Peregrine Falcon in a stoop, or dive, on prey is one of the great experiences of the outdoors. It has been recorded at speeds of up to 180 miles per hour and speeds of up to ninety miles per hour are not unusual. While these speeds do not compare with those of the Spine-tailed Swift of India, which has been recorded in level flight at 218 miles per hour over a two-mile observation, they do place the Peregrine Falcon among the fastest of the world's large birds.

The larger falcons take most of their food in the air, plunging toward small birds, ducks, gulls or other prey to strike the back with great force with their talons. The struck bird is normally grasped instantly, but sometimes falls to the ground to be retrieved. I have watched a Merlin attack from below, swooping upward after coming out of its stoop, rolling over in the air and plucking a small bird out of a flock with its talons.

Falcons that are not hungry will often hunt without killing, apparently for pleasure or practice or out of instinct. Sometimes, after roosting in a tree for some hours, they take to the air and plunge in the midst of a flock of scattering ducks, making two or three passes among them, and then flying off. This practice of killing only for food has been noted in almost all birds (foxes, on the other hand, often wipe out twenty or thirty birds in a hen house by biting off their heads).

Flying falcons can be distinguished from almost every other family of birds by their fast, determined flight, by their long wings, which are broad close to the body then taper into points, and by their long narrow tails. The tapered wings are typical of birds with a low ratio of wing expanse to body weight like sandpipers and plovers, which also fly very fast. Although under suitable conditions the larger falcons are capable of soaring, they tend to flap more than buzzards and vultures do.

Falcons range considerably in size; the Gyrfalcon, with a wingspan of about four feet, is the largest. All falcons kill from the air, although they may perch for long periods, watching for the movement of birds, rodents, small animals or even large insects. Many falcons feed extensively on smaller birds and ducks which they take in the air. In order to force its prey to fly, a falcon makes several passes overhead. Once in the air the prey is almost invariably doomed for the speed and accuracy of a hunting falcon is phenomenal. The impact of the plunging falcon striking the back of the prey sends a cloud of feathers fluttering away. Death is usually instantaneous.

The smaller species of falcons feed mostly on rodents and insects and take other small birds when they can. They hunt from perches, moving from one vantage point to another, watching and listening. These smaller falcons plunge on their prey either from a perch or from a hovering position twenty feet or so above the ground.

The story of the precipitous population decline of the Peregrine Falcon in North America and Europe is well known. Its distribution was once extensive, but its numbers are now much reduced in settled areas. Pesticides, particularly DDT, used in agriculture have made their way upward in the food chain through plants, insects, small birds and finally to the Peregrine. The result has been a toxic residue in the birds' tissues which has led to infertility and to a thinning of egg shells. By about 1970 the Peregrine had almost entirely disappeared from North America. An arctic population remains which migrates through Canada and the United States to South America. In Europe and Asia the population of Peregrines has also declined, but not to the extent it has in North America, perhaps because the use of insecticides is not as widespread at the southern end of the migratory range in Africa, southern Asia and Australia. With the banning of DDT, some recovery has taken place.

There are sixty-three species of falcons worldwide of which one-third live exclusively in Central and South America. Seven species occur in North America, six in Australia, and so on. Some are quite beautiful, my favorite being the little Nankeen Kestrel of the Far East. This pale tawny bird is frequently seen on posts in Australia. Another that is particularly attractive is the Little Falcon – also a resident of the Far East.

Left. American Kestrel (*Falco sparverius*) The American Kestrel is the smallest and most common of the falcons. In many cities, where it often nests on the ledges of tall buildings, it is credited with holding in check the population of House Sparrows.

Greater Kestrel (*Falco rupicoloides*) An African kestrel ranging locally from Ethiopia to South Africa, this species of falcon is the only one to nest in trees; the others prefer cliffs. It is much like the European Kestrel but has a dark banded tail and a white eye.

Aplomado Falcon (*Falco femoralis*) This strikingly marked falcon is now extremely rare in southern Texas and appears in small numbers as far as Tierra del Fuego. It is found in open country perching on posts. While hunting it frequently hovers.

Little Falcon (*Falco longipennis*) One of the most colorful of hawks with its rufous breast and bright blue bill, the Little Falcon is a strong and skillful hunter. It lives almost entirely on birds and is found from New Guinea to Australia.

Peregrine Falcon (*Falco peregrinus*) This Peregrine Falcon nest site – a sheltered ledge high up on a cliff – is typical. Nesting material is minimal, usually just bits of rubbish. The normal clutch is three or four eggs.

Peregrine Falcon (*Falco peregrinus*) Peregrine Falcons lay two to four reddish eggs in a clutch. One of this large family has just hatched. These birds usually nest on a sheltered ledge of a high cliff, but more and more often ledges on buildings are used.

Crested Caracara (*Caracara cheriway*) Although the Caracara feeds primarily on carrion, it does take its own food in the form of turtles, frogs, snakes, insects and fish. It is also known as the Mexican Eagle and forms the national emblem of that country.

Right. Prairie Falcon (*Falco mexicanus*) Faster than the Peregrine Falcon, the Prairie Falcon feeds on ground squirrels and other rodents as well as a variety of small birds.

American Kestrel (formerly Sparrow Hawk) (*Falco sparverius*) Kestrels use holes or cavities for nesting, some natural and some the excavations of woodpeckers. In cities they often nest in crevices in buildings, feeding well on an abundant supply of House Sparrows.

Left. American Kestrel (*Falco sparverius*) The American Kestrel prefers open grassland for hunting but needs elevated observation posts. Its numbers have expanded in the east due to clearing, and in the west due to an increased number of tree plantings and utility poles.

Merlin (formerly Pigeon Hawk) (*Falco columbarius*) This female Merlin is tending her five young which is the largest family a Merlin will have. Merlins use a variety of locations for nesting – old nests of crows and others, cliff ledges, hollows in dunes and holes in trees.

Peregrine Falcon (*Falco peregrinus*) Until recently there was a real danger that this bird would become extinct in Europe and North America. Extensive nesting and rehabilitation programs have brought it back to some extent. Arctic populations were not so badly affected.

Right. Peregrine Falcon (*Falco peregrinus*) Young Peregrine Falcons are fed fresh meat from the parent's bill. The Peregrine feeds on birds which it takes in the air. At the end of a powerful stoop or dive, it will strike its prey on the back, usually killing the bird instantly.

Merlin (formerly Pigeon Hawk) (*Falco columbarius*) This small falcon is found in the coniferous forests of the northern hemisphere. European birds migrate only locally but many North American nesters go to South America in the winter. Small birds make up the bulk of the Merlin's diet.

Right. American Kestrel (*Falco sparverius*) Male Kestrels, like this one, have blue wings and plain red tails. The females have barred red wings and black and red barred tails. Both males and females have double black sideburns.

Left. Crested Caracara (*Caracara cheriway*) A scavenger resident from Texas to Tierra del Fuego, the Crested Carcara spends most of its time walking about on its long legs. It can, however, fly strongly when it chooses and is usually found in cattle country.

Prairie Falcon (*Falco mexicanus*) The Prairie Falcon ranges widely from its cliff nest site in search of food. It seldom builds a nest, rather, it re-uses previous nest sites.

Left. Prairie Falcon (*Falcon mexicanus*) This pale falcon of the western plains of North America nests on cliffs. It flies about thirty feet above the ground while hunting.

Yellow-headed Caracara (*Milvago chimachima*) A fairly common caracara of open grasslands from Costa Rica to Argentina, this bird lives mostly on carrion. It can be seen on roads where it feeds on kills. It also picks ticks from the backs of cattle.

Peregrine Falcon (*Falco peregrinus*) Newly hatched Peregrine Falcon chicks
are an encouraging sight. Pesticide accumulation has brought this falcon
near extinction. Breeding programs in captivity are having some success,
however, in bringing their numbers back.

HAWKS

Red-tailed Hawk (*Buteo jamaicensis*) The wide range of habitats used by this bird has led it to adapt to the food available in its area. Keen eyesight allows it to hunt from a considerable height while soaring in lazy circles.

The large family of hawks known as *accipiteridae* has over two hundred species in a widely differing variety of subgroups which include the Old World vultures, kites, accipiters, buzzards (or buteos) and harriers. With all these hawks the female is larger than the male. Much confusion exists with regard to the classification of these groups and subgroups, for authorities in various parts of the world differ in their opinions, and opinions keep changing.

Confusion exists not only in classification of this wide group of hawks, varying enormously as they do in size and appearance, but also in vernacular use of their names. Buzzards, for example, are generally accepted in Europe, Africa and Asia to include the broad-winged soaring birds known in North America as buteos. The term *buzzard* is becoming accepted in North America as a replacement term for *buteo* whereas the term *buzzard* has, incorrectly, in the past been applied to the vultures.

The Old World vultures, although not of the same family as the American vultures, have certain features, such as the bald head and large wing expanse, in common with the American vultures. There are some fifteen species of Old World vultures ranging throughout southern Europe, Africa and Asia. They live entirely on carrion, both in remote and built-up areas. The bald heads and rather long necks of vultures enable them to plunge into the interior of the prey and still remain relatively clean. Old World vultures are large birds with broad wings on which they soar effortlessly in rising air, sometimes to thousands of feet. In crowded areas of India and China, they can be seen in hundreds during the day wheeling over cities. In the plains of Africa, where game is still abundant and large predators still roam, these vultures take their place in line at a kill. After the lion or leopard has had its fill, the hyenas and jackals come next, followed by the vultures, which take the remaining flesh and organs. Finally the insects have their turn, and within a day or two only white bones remain.

The group of birds known as kites consists of a number of subgroups which have several characteristics in common. Most are pale in appearance or at least have a pale head, underside or tail. They are all excellent fliers with a tendency to hover over their prey with feet dangling. Many take their prey in the air and feed while still flying, but all kites snatch up their prey with their feet. The Brahminy Kite of India and eastwards can be seen in large numbers over villages and cities swooping and diving. It scavenges to some extent, but at garbage dumps it provides a service in taking large numbers of rats and mice. The Lammergeyer, with a wingspan of eight to ten feet, is the largest of the kites. It lives in the mountains and feeds largely on carrion, often taking the bones which it swallows whole after vultures have cleaned off the flesh.

The group known as accipiters is that from which the hawk family takes its name. It consists of some forty species and occurs throughout the temperate and tropical world with the exception of the islands of the Pacific and New Zealand. Accipiters are good hunters and agile fliers. They have rounded, rather short wings, long tails and long bald shanks. They are, for the most part, forest birds, hunting from perches high in the trees from which they dash to take small mammals and birds. The Goshawk is the largest of the accipiters. It breeds in northern areas around the world, and although it is still quite common in Europe and Asia, it is now rare in North America.

Buzzards are hunters but they fill a different niche from falcons and accipiters in that they are not as adept at killing or as swift. They live for the most part on reptiles and small mammals which are easier to catch than are birds. Their service to man is inestimable for in many areas they feed largely on rats and mice.

Another subfamily of hawks is represented by seventeen species of harriers or marsh hawks, so called for their common habit of flying a few feet above marshes, meadows and prairies, quartering back and forth in search of frogs, birds, insects and rodents. Because they fly so close to the ground, usually above dense marsh growth, their range of vision is limited, forcing them to rely to some extent on sound. All have owl-like facial disks which probably reflect the sound of the scurrying of their prey to their ears. In North America the only species at present is the Northern Harrier, known in Europe as the Hen Harrier, which is quickly identifiable by its long rounded wings and long square tail with a clear white patch at the base.

Great Black Hawk (*Buteogallus urubitinga*) The range of this large hawk extends from Mexico to Uruguay. It is never far from water, hunting for its prey near streams and sometimes over mangrove swamps.

Red-tailed Hawk (*Buteo jamaicensis*) This North American hawk is common almost everywhere on the continent. In most color phases it is easily distinguished by the reddish tail, which is unbarred except for a narrow band at the tip.

Broad-winged Hawk (*Buteo platypterus*) This hawk is seldom seen in the open other than while on migration, for it prefers to remain deep in the forest. It feeds on toads, frogs, some small birds and on a variety of large insects.

Nest of Broad-winged Hawk (*Buteo platypterus*) The nest of the Broad-winged Hawk is usually built close to the trunk of a large tree and is kept decorated by green foliage. This hawk lives in the deciduous forests of North America.

Auger Buzzard (*Buteo rufofoscus*) This buzzard feeds exclusively on rodents.

Sharp-shinned Hawk (*Accipiter striatus*) This hawk lays its eggs in a nest of twigs in a woodland tree. The laying of the eggs is timed so that the fully-fledged young leave the nest in time to practice their hunting skills on the young of songbirds.

Right. Sharp-shinned Hawk (*Accipiter striatus*) This accipiter, which is smaller than the similar Cooper's Hawk, nests over most of North America, wintering south to Guatemala. It feeds entirely on small birds and can usually be identified by its long narrow tail.

Mountain Hawk-eagle (*Spizaetus nipalensis*) This large eagle normally sits against a screen of foliage while waiting for prey, but in the mornings it may soar for an hour or two. It is found in the highlands of southeast Asia.

Right. Zone-tailed Hawk (*Buteo albonotatus*) This black bird bears some resemblance to the larger Turkey Vulture. This similarity may fool some of its prey into thinking they have nothing to fear from a bird that eats only carrion.

Ferruginous Hawk (*Buteo regalis*)
A Ferruginous Hawk in its nest.
This bird appears in two color
phases – light and dark. The dark
phase shows deep brown under
the wings and undersides. This
one is in its light phase.

Ferruginous Hawk (*Buteo regalis*)
When searching for its food of
ground squirrels, rabbits and
rodents, this hawk flies close to
the ground or perches in
prominent places. Despite its
value to farmers, it is often
heedlessly shot.

Ferruginous Hawk (*Buteo regalis*) A common large hawk of the plains of western Canada and the United States, the Ferruginous Hawk often can be seen soaring over fields.

Pale Chanting Goshawk (*Melierax poliopterus*) The pose shown here is uncharacteristic, for this long-legged hawk usually sits upright. The name comes from its piping call; most hawks cry, shriek or have rasping calls.

Pages 78-79. Rough-legged Hawk (*Buteo lagopus*) A Rough-legged Hawk looks out from its Arctic nest. Like the Snowy Owl, this hawk will lay more eggs in years when lemmings and other food are abundant. It is the only hawk to breed exclusively in the Arctic.

Cooper's Hawk (*Accipiter cooperii*) This, and the similar Sharp-shinned Hawk, can be recognized in flight by their short rounded wings and long narrow tail, and by their habit of flapping their wings four or five times and then gliding.

Cooper's Hawk (*Accipiter cooperii*) This hawk builds a nest of twigs and sticks into a bulky platform, usually at least twenty feet above ground. It usually lays four eggs.

Cooper's Hawk (*Accipiter cooperii*) Pesticides have diminished the number of Cooper's Hawks as they have Peregrine Falcons. This hawk is now gone from the eastern deciduous forests of North America.

Goshawk (*Accipiter gentilis*) This bird is fearless in defense of its nest, which it usually builds in a tree. It will attack anyone who ventures too close.

Right. Harris' Hawk (*Parabuteo unicinctus*) Ranging from the southern United States to South America, this hawk is often seen perched on telephone or power poles along the highway. It preys on snakes, rabbits, quail and lizards.

Northern Harrier (formerly Marsh Hawk) (*Circus cyaneus*) This hawk hunts by flying close to the ground and taking its prey by surprise. Its disk-shaped face is thought to amplify sound and aid it in finding its prey.

Red-tailed Hawk (*Buteo jamaicensis*) A resident of forests and nearby open country, this hawk builds its nest – a large structure of sticks lined with bark and vegetation – in a tall tree or on a rock ledge.

Right. Ornate Hawk-eagle (*Spizaetus ornatus*) This beautiful hawk is noted for the rich color of its collar and nape and for the spiky crest which is elevated when the bird is disturbed. It is an uncommon bird, found in forests from Mexico to Argentina.

Spotted Harrier (*Circus assimilis*) The Spotted Harrier, which is native to Australia, Tasmania and the Celebes, has long legs with bare shanks. It glides over paddocks and open country searching for small birds and mammals.

Northern Harrier (formerly Marsh Hawk) (*Circus cyaneus*) The Northern Harrier has a facial disk of smooth feathers much like an owl's. The disk reflects the sounds of prey to its ears, thus aiding the bird in its hunting.

Swainson's Hawk (*Buteo swainsoni*) This Swainson's Hawk is in the dark phase. Those in the light phase have pale underwings and bellies and dark throats. This hawk nests in western North America and winters south to Argentina.

Mississippi Kite (*Ictinia mississippiensis*) This uncommon kite frequents brushy pastures and open woods, darting about like a swallow in search of prey. In summer it wanders north to southern Canada and in winter ranges south to Argentina.

Everglade Kite (*Rostrhamus sociabilis*) This South American kite lives in fresh water swamps where it feeds on only one species of snail. Once, many of these kites lived in Florida but now only a few birds remain. Their highly specific feeding requirements have limited their numbers.

White-backed Vulture (*Pseudogyps africanus*) White-backed Vultures in East Africa take their turn at carrion in the big game country after the lions and other killing animals have had their fill.

White-backed Vulture (*Pseudogyps africanus*) This large vulture, unlike most of its kind which nest on cliffs, builds a nest in trees in the forest or in the trees that line watercourses in Africa. It has a conspicuous white rump.

Egyptian Vulture (*Neophron pernopterus*) This small vulture of the
northeastern part of Africa from Tanzanya northward, has a distinctive
wedge-shaped white tail. It is found around Masai villages where it feeds on
the leavings.

Lappet-faced Vulture (*Torgos tracheliotus*) The Lappet-faced is the largest of the African vultures. The body is dark brown, the head, as can be seen, is reddish purple. It is uncommon but widespread from North Africa to South Africa. It is best seen in big game areas.

Overleaf. Hooded Vulture (*Necrosyrtes monachus*) The smallest of the African vultures, these birds are common in Uganda, Kenya and Tanzanya. They are one of the few birds that have no call.

Ruppell's Griffon Vulture (*Gyps rupellii*) This is a medium-sized vulture of East and West Africa. The creamy margins of the wing coverts show clearly and give the bird a mottled appearance.

EAGLES

Martial Eagle (*Poleamaetus bellicosus*) This massive African eagle lives up to the second part of its scientific name *bellicosus* for it preys on monkeys, rock hyrax and even on small antelopes. Its rounded crest is not always visible.

Eagles belong to the hawk family and form a subgroup of the buzzards or buteos. Of the 226 species of birds that are classified as hawks, some fifty-nine species are recognized as eagles. However, some birds that are called eagles should not be so named. The Australian Whistling Eagle is really a kite, and the insectivorous Grasshopper Buzzard Eagle of Africa is a buzzard.

There are four recognized groups of eagles:

The members of the first group, known as sea eagles, feed mostly on fish they catch themselves. The largest sea eagles are the European Sea Eagle and the Stellar's Sea Eagle, the smallest is the Lesser Fishing Eagle, which lives in the forests of the Far East. One member of this family is known as the Palm Nut Vulture or the Vulturine Fish Eagle. It feeds mostly on the fruit of the oil palm.

The second group are the serpent or snake eagles. These birds are found soaring rather fast on broad wings over plains and marshes. As their name suggests, they feed almost entirely on snakes and other reptiles. They have large yellow eyes and thicker toes than other eagles, giving them the power to immobilize their prey quickly. This ability is essential, for eagles are not immune to snake venom. The Bateleur Eagle of Africa has been called the "flying wing" for in flight its short tail does not extend beyond the line of its body. It is capable of acrobatic tumbling in the air.

The next group of eagles, the so-called crested and solitary eagles of South America, is closely related to the buzzards. It includes the Harpy, the largest of all the eagles, which feeds on monkeys and sloths in the jungles of the Amazon.

The largest group, comprising thirty species, consists of the booted eagles, whose legs are feathered to the feet.

Most people think of eagles as monstrous, fierce-looking birds that carry off young lambs. Some are, but many species are the same size as other hawks and take relatively small prey and insects. It is the large eagles that attract the most attention. The Golden Eagle lives in remote areas throughout the Northern Hemisphere and is seldom seen near settled areas. Each pair demands an extensive hunting ground, usually in the mountains, both in its nesting area and, when it migrates, in its winter territory. Not only does it keep its territory clear of its own kind, it often drives out or kills other predators. It is this species that has been trained to kill animals as large as wolves.

The Bald Eagle, symbol of the United States, is exclusively a North American species, nesting from Alaska southward. The eastern population was declared to be endangered in the 1970s because of the drastic reduction in its numbers due to ingestion of pesticides. In recent years, its numbers have recovered somewhat. On the west coast, the Bald Eagle is still numerous, particularly along the wild shoreline. One morning I saw six birds flying together on Vancouver Island. This eagle is not very predaceous, feeding mostly on dead fish which it finds along the shore, but occasionally it takes ducks on the water, after forcing them to dive until they are exhausted.

The king of the eagles is the Harpy, probably the world's most powerful bird. The female is, as with all birds of prey, larger than the male, and weighs up to twenty pounds. Its lower legs, which are as thick as a child's wrist, end in toes that span nine inches with talons of one and a half inches. This huge bird lives in the forest and is one of the few hawks that does not soar, although it is probably capable of doing so. The very large African Crowned Eagle, for instance, is a regular soarer and has been known to kill antelopes of thirty pounds.

Among the sea eagles the Stellar's is the largest and most striking. It has a pattern of black and white feathers and an arched yellow bill. It lives in Siberia and along the coast of the northwestern Pacific. This bird feeds on salmon, some birds and even young seals.

One of the great sights on the plains of Africa is a Martial Eagle circling and swooping in the clear sky. This bird with an eight-foot wingspan has been recorded taking bushbuck of thirty-five pounds.

Eagles are long-lived birds. Unless a wild bird is banded, its age cannot be determined. However, captive birds have been known to live for up to fifty-five years. And it would appear from an analysis of population and reproduction statistics that wild birds may be expected to survive from twenty to forty years.

Bald Eagle (*Haliaeetus leucocephalus*) Primarily a fish-eater, the Bald Eagle will also prey on water fowl and carrion. Only the adults, those over five years old, have the characteristic white head, neck and tail. Until then, the body is mostly brown.

Bald Eagle (*Haliaeetus leucocephalus*) Young Bald Eagles do not grow the white feathers on the head and neck until they are four or five years old and gain breeding maturity. Pairs appear to mate for life and nest in the same area each year, although they may build several nests.

Bald Eagle (*Haliaeetus leucocephalus*) Formerly classified as an endangered species, the Bald Eagle has made a recovery since the use of the most toxic pesticides was discontinued in North America. The Bald Eagle is the emblem of the United States of America.

Left. Black (Verreaux's) Eagle (*Aquila verreauxii*) In Africa, from the Sudan to South Africa, this rare eagle hunts from rocky crags and cliffs. Despite its name, it has a white rump and black and pale patches on the flight feathers.

Bateleur (*Terathopius ecaudatus*) This eagle is found throughout the plains and savannah woodlands of both east and west Africa. It has a remarkably short tail which in flight is scarcely visible.

Golden Eagle (*Aquila chrysaētos*) The Golden Eagle lives throughout the northern hemisphere, always in remote areas. Each pair requires an extensive territory for hunting which they protect from other eagles and often from competing hawks and owls as well.

Golden Eagle (*Aquila chrysaëtos*)
The Golden Eagle is much reduced in numbers throughout its range in part because there are fewer wilderness areas and in part because it has been accused of taking domesticated animals. A very few birds do take lambs and young pigs but the amount of damage has been exaggerated.

Golden Eagle (*Aquila chrysaëtos*)
A Golden Eagle feeds on a marmot which it has just killed. These eagles also eat groundhogs and foxes as well as skunks and cats.

Left. Bald Eagle (*Haliaeetus leucocephalus*) For such a magnificent bird, the Bald Eagle has a weak, thin voice.

Nest of a Bald Eagle (*Haliaeetus leucocephalus*) Built in the main crotch of a living tree, this Bald Eagle nest has grown to enormous size. Year after year, the eagles add to the nest until it eventually becomes so large that it may damage or even destroy the tree.

African Fish Eagle (*Cuncuma vocifer*) The cry of this eagle is a recollection that travelers bring back from Africa. This large chestnut, black and white bird is found mostly near water preying on fish, but it also takes rodents.

OWLS

Little Owl (*Athene noctua*) A resident in the northern half of the United Kingdom and throughout Europe south of Scandinavia, the Little Owl is often seen in daylight perching on wires or poles where it bobs up and down when nervous.

Most people have seen owls only in photographs or films or on television, although they may have heard owls call in the night. Most owl species roost as unobtrusively as possible during the day and emerge toward dusk to hunt. They continue hunting intermittently during the night, and become more active again around dawn. There are a number of species such as the Short-eared Owl, found in Europe, Asia, and North and South America, that hunt by day as well as by night. In years when lemmings are scarce, the Snowy Owl and the Great Gray Owl drift south from the Arctic into the more settled areas of Europe, Asia and North America.

There are owls in almost every part of the world with the exception of Antarctica. They are divided into two families: the barn owls, *tytonidae*, of which there are nine species, and the others, *strigidae*, of which there are about 126 species. Of these latter, ten have wide distribution covering more than one continent, thirty-four occur in the Far East including the islands of the Pacific, twenty are restricted to Africa, forty occur only in North and South America, and twenty-two have restricted distribution, usually on remote islands or in mountainous areas. Of the nine species of barn owls, five have only a limited distribution, three are widespread in the Far East, and one, the Barn Owl, *tytoalba*, appears in almost all parts of the world.

The common features of owls are the varyingly pronounced facial disk, which reflects the tiny sounds of scurrying mammals to the owls' ears, and the large eyes, which are effective in minimal amounts of light. With only a few exceptions owls have short tails which, with their large heads, contribute to their chunky appearance. While hawks have stiff feathers which are noisy in flight, owls' feathers are soft, enabling them to fly almost silently. Most species become active at dusk when they fly off in search of food. It is then, and during the night, that one can hear the hoots, toots and screeches that identify the various species.

Owls for the most part swallow their prey whole or in large chunks which include hair and bone. The digestive system then accepts as nourishment the edible material and forms pellets of fur and bone which are regurgitated. These pellets accumulate at the base of the roosting or nesting tree and can be used by bird watchers as a guide for finding owls.

Owls tend to be less migratory than most other birds except when a decline in their food supply forces them into new areas. These movements tend to be periodic, usually over a four- or five-year cycle. Migration within the family occurs when the young of the year are fledged and become independent. They are then forced out of the hunting area by their parents.

The saying that owls can see in the dark is, of course, incorrect, for no animal can see without some light. What is unusual about owls is that during a long period of evolution they have developed large eyes which are particularly adapted to gather maximum amounts of both direct and reflected light. The light gathered in the lens is passed to the retina, the retina being closer to the lens than in the eyes of humans.

The eyes of owls, unlike those of almost all other birds, are at the front of the head, looking forward. With most birds the eyes are at the sides of the head, giving them a separate range of vision for each eye, but not the same one for both eyes at the same time. Additionally, the eyes of owls are fixed in their sockets, requiring the owl to constantly turn its head to change its field of vision. The neck is so adapted that the head can turn up to 270 degrees in either direction.

To aid the owl's ability to hunt at night, the evolutionary process has added an extraordinarily acute sense of hearing. The owl's auricular openings are much larger than those in other birds, and its flat facial disk reflects the sounds to these openings. Owls can thereby hear even the slightest movements or squeaks of their prey.

Most owls feed on rodents and larger mammals, although some of the smaller species snap up flying insects with their bills. The animal-hunting species strike with their claws extended in front of the body at the moment of impact. Some, such as the fishing owls of Africa and Asia, as their name implies, feed almost exclusively on fish.

Owls follow a wide range of nesting habits. Some, such as the Great Horned Owl of the Western Hemisphere, use the existing nests of other large birds like hawks; apparently these owls never build their own nests; they just add to old ones. Others, such as the Snowy Owl, nest on the ground, usually scooping out a shallow depression and filling it with twigs and down. A number of species of burrowing owls use prairie dog or ground squirrel tunnels. Many species use holes in trees or occasionally manmade bird boxes. Some individuals of several species nest in structures such as bridges and culverts or abandoned buildings.

Flammulated Owl (*Otus flammeolus*) This tiny owl lives in the highlands of the western United States south to Guatemala, almost invariably in evergreens. It may be either gray or rusty in color and is the only small owl with dark brown eyes.

Right. Boreal Owl (*Aegolius funerea*) This little owl breeds in the northern forests of North America, Asia and Europe. Some move into more southerly areas in winter. They are quite tame and frequently can be found in abandoned buildings.

Left. Great Horned Owl (*Bubo virginianus*) In feeding its young the Great Horned Owl brings every kind of animal matter to the nest including large insects, birds such as hawks and owls, and animals. Rabbits are its chief food where they are available.

Great Horned Owl (*Bubo virginianus*) These young birds have left the nest but are not yet independent. The young are paler on the breast than mature birds and are rusty in color. The ear tufts have not yet grown.

Great Gray Owl (*Strix nebulosa*) At the moment of attack all owls, like this Great Gray Owl, thrust their feet forward to grasp their prey. Usually, the prey is carried away in their talons but sometimes it is eaten on the ground.

Great Gray Owl (*Strix nebulosa*) This owl prefers coniferous forests, and it nests in northern regions around the world. During hard winters in the north it wanders into populated areas where it will usually allow an observer to approach quite closely.

Northern Eagle Owl (*Bubo bubo*) This large European owl can be seen only in remote areas where it prefers rocky headlands and crags. The "ears" may be erect, as pictured here, or held flat, projecting from the sides of the head.

Right. Boreal Owl (*Aegolius funerea*) Easily confused with the Saw-whet Owl, which has a dark bill, the Boreal Owl is entirely nocturnal. It spends the day in hollow trees or dense spruce.

Great Gray Owl (*Strix nebulosa*)
This large northern owl hunts
during the day. A resident of
forest and muskeg, it nests in
trees and lays two to five eggs.

Long-eared Owl (*Asio otus*) This
owl is particularly violent in
defense of its nest. To protect its
young, it will assume a
threatening posture with its wings
fanned over its back.

Long-eared Owl (*Asio otus*) This nocturnal owl lives in the forests of North America where in winter it forms groups of about twenty-five birds. They are seldom seen for they are quiet during the day and are unlikely to flush from their roosts.

121

Left. Saw-whet Owl (*Aegolius acadicus*) This small, tame owl hunts at night, preying on mice and other small rodents. It nests in holes in trees.

Short-eared Owl (*Asio flammeus*) This owl, which is broadly distributed in North and South America, Asia and Europe, can often be seen hunting by day over pastures, marshes and dunes. Short-eared Owls often form fairly large groups that hunt together.

Great Horned Owl (*Bubo virginianus*) This owl does not make its own nest; instead, it uses old ones of other large birds such as hawks and herons. It also nests on ledges, in caves, in hollow trees and on the supports of bridges.

Right. Great Horned Owl (*Bubo virginianus*) This owl is found all over the western hemisphere. It nests in cities and should be approached with caution for it often attacks intruders. It feeds on animals as large as skunks.

Left. Hawk-owl (*Surnia ulula*) The Hawk-owl is well adapted to its northern home. It hunts during the daytime, feeding on rodents in the summer and birds in winter. Its long tail and swift flight resemble those of a hawk.

Saw-whet Owl (*Aegolius acadicus*) This little owl got its name from its call, which sounds like a saw being filed. It also makes an upslurred whistle.

Snowy Owl (*Nyctea scandiaca*) The Snowy Owl is more active during the day than most other owls. In the Arctic it feeds on lemmings, hares, ptarmigan and fish. It nests on the ground and lines the nest with feathers and moss.

Right. Snowy Owl (*Nyctea scandiaca*) This almost white owl of the Arctic is circumpolar. In winters when there are few lemmings it comes south in large numbers and can be seen in daylight sitting on poles or on hayricks.

Left. Snowy Owl (*Nyctea scandiaca*) The amount of barring on the breasts of Snowy Owls varies considerably. This one is darker than most. In winter, Snowy Owls spend much of their time perched high up.

Burrowing Owl (*Athene cunicularia*) This small owl is found in open country. It nests in colonies of up to twelve pairs, often in the abandoned dens of prairie dogs or other burrowing animals. It is also found in open areas, like airports, in cities.

Left. Spotted Owl (*Strix occidentalis*) A resident of the western United States and Mexico, this rare bird is much like the Barred Owl of the east. It lives in the forests at fairly high elevations and perches by day close to the trunk of a tree.

Short-eared Owl (*Asio flammeus*) A medium-sized owl, the Short-eared Owl is at home in open country with short vegetation. It hunts for field mice and small rodents, patrolling in flight or perched on a stump.

Left. Barred Owl (*Strix varia*) A big grayish-brown owl of the swamps and deep forests, the Barred Owl is found from northern Canada to Honduras. It is often heard calling its eight hoots in two separate groups of four.

Barred Owl (*Strix varia*) This owl does not have the ferocity or strength of the Great Horned Owl, and its feet are relatively week. As a consequence its prey is limited to mice, rats, insects and frogs.

Ferruginous Pygmy-Owl (*Glaucidium brasilianum*) The range of this tiny owl extends from Texas to the Straits of Magellan. Only six inches long, it has a realtively small head and is noted for its habit of flipping its longish tail.

Screech Owl (*Otus asio*) A Screech Owl returns to its nesting hole with a large moth. This owl nests from Canada to Mexico in natural cavities in trees, woodpecker holes and in birdhouses. In addition to moths, it eats birds, bats and small mammals.

BARN OWLS

Left. Great Horned Owl (*Bubo virginianus*) The widely spaced, horn-shaped tufts at the sides of the Great Horned Owl's head are the predominent markings of this strong, ferocious and silent hunter of the woods.

Barn Owl (*Tyto alba*) The Barn Owl's facial disk reflects the tiny sounds of prey to the owl's ears, thus helping it locate its quarry in the dark.

The nine barn owl species form a family distinct from the typical owls. The one that gives its name to the family is known scientifically as *tytoalba*. It has an almost universal distribution throughout the temperate world, although some minor subspecific differences occur in different areas. This bird is almost white below and darker on top. As with all barn owl species it has long legs, thinly feathered to the toes, and a distinct heart-shaped facial disk. Barn owls are strictly nocturnal. They have adapted to settled areas, roosting and nesting extensively in farm buildings where they are usually welcomed by farmers for they feed on mice and rats. In remote areas they will nest in holes in trees or crevices in rock faces.

In some towns in tropical or semitropical regions, barn owls may be present in some numbers. At night they can be attracted by squeaking noises made by the observer.

Barn Owl (*Tyto alba*) Although it nests on flat surfaces, the Barn Owl needs trees for perching. It sits upright on long feathered legs.

Bay Owl (*Phodilus badius*) The Bay Owl is one of the family of nine Barn Owls. About the size of a pigeon, it is found infrequently throughout southeast Asia.

Bay Owl (*Phodilus badius*) The family of Barn Owls are all pale in color and have elongated faces. This Bay Owl is distributed throughout southeast Asia.

Barn Owl (*Tyto alba*) A Barn Owl protects its young. These owls nest at almost any time of the year for they live only in fairly temperate or warm climates. They lay up to eleven eggs in a clutch, although not all the young will survive to maturity.

Barn Owl (*Tyto alba*) The Barn Owl probably has the widest distribution of any bird, for it is found virtually worldwide. It lays its eggs in almost any dark and sheltered place but it makes no nest.

PHOTO CREDITS

Fred Bruemmer, 78-79
Pauline and Ralph Brunner, 69
Richard Fyfe, 4-5, 11, 64
Dr. Donald R. Gunn, 23, 33, 122
Tom W. Hall, 51, 65, 104, 105 (bottom)
Dr. Cy Hampson, 10, 49, 70 (top)
Bill Ivy, 100 (bottom)
Edgar T. Jones, 44, 55, 58, 60, 69, 75, 80, 81 (top), 84 (top), 114, 119, 126

Thomas W. Kitchin, 36, 38, 50, 59, 88, 129
Wayne Lynch, 9, 34, 90, 91, 92, 96
George K. Peck, 8, 16, 35, 61, 76, 77 (bottom), 87, 105 (top), 107, 118, 121, 139, 142 (top)
R. Barry Ranford, 21, 24, 25, 31, 37, 40, 52-53, 81 (bottom), 83, 84 (bottom), 100 (top), 123, 124, 127, 130, 133, 134, 140

Richard D. Robinson, 41, 56, 115, 125, 142 (bottom)
Dennis W. Schmidt, 26-27
J.D. Taylor, 28, 57, 101, 117
Jack Templeton, 131, 138
Diane Winter, 20
Bob and Peter Wood, 48, 54, 62, 70 (bottom), 72, 77 (top), 82, 113, 116, 120, 128, 135
Leonard Zorn, 32, 106, 137

From The National Audubon Society Collection/PR-Miller Services:

Stephen Dalton, 109
Kenneth W. Fink, 102, 141 (left)
Ray Gilbert, 29
François Gohier, 68, 136
Jose L.G. Grande, 97
Samuel Grimes, 89 (bottom)
Ken M. Highfill, 89 (top)

M. Philip Kahl, Jr., 94-95
Russ Kinene, 19, 46
Gary Ladd, 132
Tom McHugh, 39, 47, 74, 85, 103
Anthony Mercieca, 141 (right)
Lawrence E. Naylor, 63
Richard Parker, 17

Mark N. Boulton, 71,
William Ray, 112
Mitch Readon, 45
Leonard Lee Rue, 93
Frank Schreider, 2
Marshall Sklar, 108
Peter Slater, 86

PHOTO INDEX